Introduction

The Greeks you will read about in this book lived 2500 years ago. That is 500 years before Jesus Christ was born. We write this as 500 **BC**. The letters B and C mean Before Christ. They are called the **Ancient** Greeks because they lived such a very long time ago.

The Ancient Greeks lived thousands of years ago but we know a lot about them. We have **evidence** like these vases which show us what the Greeks wore and some of the things they did.

You can also visit the wonderful buildings they built.

In this book you will find other kinds of evidence telling you about the Greeks.

ACTIVITIES

1 What are the people doing in the vase pictures?

2 Paint your own vase pictures to show what things people do today. You could use an orange wash and paint over it in black.

3 Collect holiday brochures showing pictures of Greece. What picture evidence can you find? What can you find out about the Greek weather and countryside?

Greek Cities

The Ancient Greeks lived in different cities which were like small countries. They were called **city states**.

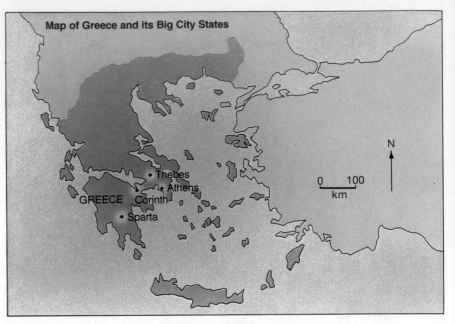

Map of Greece and its Big City States

Sparta and Athens

Two of the biggest city states were Sparta and Athens.

Spartan soldiers were famous fighters. All Spartan boys went to an army school when they were seven where they were trained to be tough and brave. They were often whipped to teach them to stand pain.

Spartan girls trained and kept fit like the boys. A Greek called Xenophon wrote this:

Other Greeks required girls sitting still and working wool . . . . how should girls like this be expected to have strong babies?

Athens also had a strong army but only boys trained to fight. Rich boys also learnt lessons in reading, writing, athletics and music. Girls had to stay at home and help their mothers.

▲ Statue of a Spartan girl running.

A view of Athens.

At first all the city states were ruled by one man who had to be obeyed by everyone. Some people did not like this and the **government** changed in many of the towns.

By 500 BC Sparta was ruled by a group of old men called a council. When they had to decide what to do they voted by shouting 'yes' or 'no'. The loudest shout won!

Athens was very different. It became a **democracy**. Men over eighteen could vote. They met together to decide what should happen in Athens and elect people in the government. Women could not vote.

ACTIVITIES

1 Look at the picture of the Spartan soldier and describe it.

2 People from Athens thought Spartan girls were rude because they wore short tunics and acted like men. What do you think?

3 How did the government in Athens change?

4 What does the word democracy mean? Could everyone in Athens vote? Write down the good and bad things about democracy in Athens.

Statue of a Spartan soldier.

Land and Trade

The first towns were often built on hills. The farmers grew food for the city states. They grew crops in the valleys and kept sheep and goats on the hills. But it was difficult to farm because the land was dry and rocky.

Some cities got very crowded. Farmers could not grow enough food to feed all the people. Then the cities sent out explorers to look for new lands across the sea. There they built new towns for their people to live in. These new lands were called **colonies.**

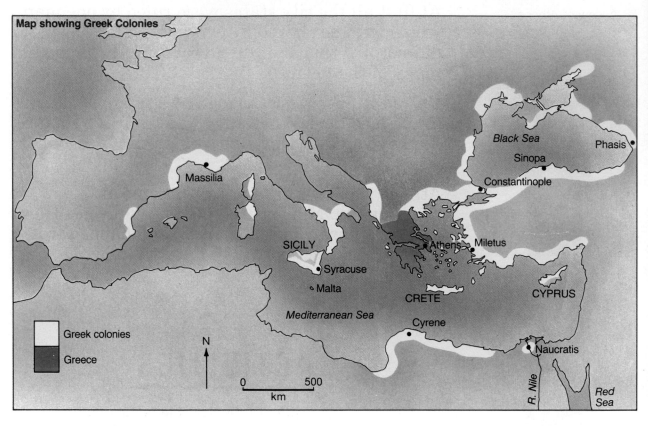

Map showing Greek Colonies

Black Sea
Phasis
Sinopa
Constantinople
Massilia
SICILY
Athens
Miletus
Syracuse
Malta
CYPRUS
CRETE
Mediterranean Sea
Cyrene
Naucratis
R. Nile
Red Sea

Greek colonies
Greece

N

0   500
km

Trade

The new lands meant that the Greeks could sell things to more people and buy what they needed more easily. This **trade** was good for Greece. The Greeks sold wine, pottery and olive oil to other countries. This gave them the money to buy the grain they needed from Egypt.

At first the Greeks did not have real money. They paid for things and bought them with short iron bars. With all the extra trade they began to use coins called drachmas.

The Greeks now had to travel by sea to trade with other countries. This could be dangerous. Sometimes ships were wrecked on the rocks or by rough seas. Trading ships were also attacked by pirate ships as is shown on this vase.

ACTIVITIES

1 What were the new Greek colonies and why did the Greeks need them?

2 Look at the map showing Greek colonies. Use your atlas to make a list of modern countries which once had Greek colonies.

3 The new colonies led to more trade. What else changed?

Greece and Persia

Persia was a country far from Greece. It had a large **empire**.

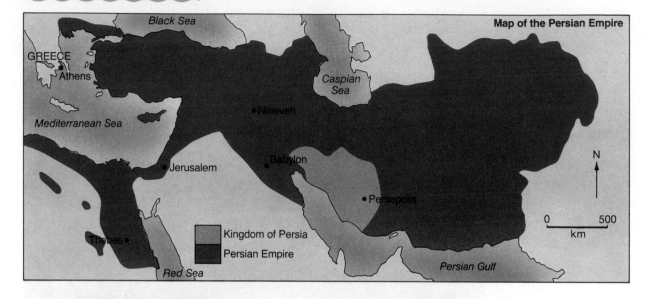

Map of the Persian Empire

Black Sea

GREECE
Athens

Mediterranean Sea

Caspian Sea

Nineveh

Jerusalem

Babylon

Persepolis

Thebes

Kingdom of Persia
Persian Empire

Red Sea

Persian Gulf

N

0   500
km

▲ This vase shows a Greek soldier fighting with a Persian soldier.

Greek colonies were often attacked by the Persians and Athens sent soldiers to help them. A Greek writer, Herodotus, said that when the colonies asked for help they wrote this to the Greeks.

The Persians are an unwarlike people; and you are the best and bravest warriors in the whole world. They are so easy to beat.

The Greeks could not stop the Persian armies. The Persians attacked Greece. Sparta and Athens joined together to fight them.

In 492 BC King Darius of Persia ordered the Greeks to obey him. But in 490 BC his army was defeated at the Battle of Marathon.

In 481 BC Xerxes, another Persian king, left to attack Greece. He had a huge army and navy. Herodotus wrote:

> The number of foot soldiers was 170 000. That of the horsemen was 80 000 to which must be added the Arabs who rode on camels, and the Libyans who fought in chariots whom I reckon at 20 000.

Athens was captured. Its buildings were burnt and destroyed. But the Greeks beat the Persian fleet of ships in 480 BC and finally defeated the Persian army in 479 BC. The Persians had to leave Greece and peace was made in 449 BC.

After the war with Persia Athens became the most important and powerful city in Greece.

ACTIVITIES

1 Do you think the colonies wrote the truth? Were the Persians 'easy to beat'? Why do you think they would lie to the people of Athens when they needed help?

2 Write a description of the Greek and Persian soldiers and draw the two soldiers fighting.

3 Herodotus was one of the first people to write down what happened. Could we learn as much about the wars from the vase pictures?

4 Do you think the rulers of Sparta were happy that Athens became more powerful than they were? What do you think might happen?

Beautiful Buildings

▲ The ruins of the Parthenon with a model of what it was like when it was built.

A great temple called the Parthenon was built in Athens.

The Parthenon was built at the top of the Acropolis where the old town had been. Large blocks of marble were cut out of the ground in quarries. Most of the stone was moved on carts or sledges. New roads had to be built. Huge pillars of stone had wheels put on them at each end. It took about two days to get each block of stone to Athens. The stone was dragged up the hillside on wooden rollers. At the top men cut the stone into shape.

The temple was built between 448 BC and 433 BC. Many people worked on it: including miners, road-makers, shoe-makers, carpenters, stone-cutters, painters and goldsmiths.

A great sculptor called Pheidias made five hundred statues and carvings to decorate the Parthenon. Inside he made a huge statue of Athena, the goddess of Athens. The statue was about fourteen metres high and her eyes were made of precious jewels.

A Greek writer called Pausanius saw the statue and wrote:

. . . . this work is in ivory and gold . . . the statue of Athena is full length, with a tunic reaching to her knees . . . in one hand she has a Victory four cubits high and in the other a spear, and at her feet a shield, and near the spear a snake.

This drawing shows the statue of Athena as it was.

This is a picture of the statue's shield. One of the men may be Pheidias himself.

ACTIVITIES

1 Some of the wheels used to move the pillars were four metres high. Measure this on the floor. Do you think this is the same size as the wheels of a car or lorry?

2 Draw a series of pictures to show how the stone and pillars got from the quarry to the top of the Acropolis and were made into the temple.

3 Choose three of the people who worked on the temple. What do you think they did to help build it?

4 Why do you think Pheidias put his picture on the shield?

5 The Greeks used pillars and columns to hold up roofs. Have you seen any buildings which remind you of a Greek temple?

Daily Life

Home and family

Greek houses were built with bricks and mud. In the towns they were small but people built larger houses in the country. These farmhouses were built around a garden where the family could relax. Most houses did not have a lot of furniture. **Archaeologists** have found cooking pots like these which were used in Greek kitchens.

Men often worked in farming, trade or in the army. Most Greek women had to obey the men. In Athens women could not buy their own homes. Girls were not often allowed out of the house. A Roman visitor to Athens wrote,

> The wife is never at dinner unless it is a family party and she spends all her time in the women's part of the house where a man can only go if he is a close relative.

Girls were told by their fathers whom they had to marry. Once they were married women had to obey their husbands. They had to stay at home and work.

▲ This vase shows a woman spinning.

It was different for men. They visited each other to eat and drink. Dancing girls entertained them.

▶ A vase showing men being entertained at a dinner party.

Both Greek men and women wore tunics. Most women wore tunics called **chitons** like those on this vase.

▲ This statue shows the himation.

In the winter men and women wore cloaks called **himations.** They were made of wool. Outside, people wore sandals. In their homes they went barefooted.

Women tried many different hair styles. Sometimes they dyed their hair. Sometimes they used curlers. Some women even wore wigs. Rich women also wore beautiful jewellery.

▶ Greek jewellery.

▼ A Greek hairstyle.

Slaves

People were bought by rich families to be **slaves.** The slaves had to work for and obey their owners. Most slaves were brought to Greece from other countries and some very rich men owned hundreds of slaves. The slaves had to buy the food in the market and get it ready for eating.

▶ A woman baking.

◀ A slave helping her mistress with her shoe.

Sometimes slaves were used as teachers for their master's children. There were thousands of slaves in Athens. Some had to work in the mines. There the work was hard and dangerous. The mines were dark and hot and the only light came from candles.

ACTIVITIES

1 Did the Athenians treat women fairly? Why?

2 From what you read on page 4 do you think Spartan women were treated in the same way?

3 We can tell a lot about Greek clothes from the paintings and statues the Greeks made. How will people in the future know about the fashions we have today?

4 Use an old sheet or piece of cloth to wear a tunic or a cloak like the Greeks.

5 Draw a picture of a Greek woman using all the evidence in this book showing what she is wearing, her hair and her jewellery.

6 Most Greeks could see nothing wrong with slavery. What do you think?

Greek Gods

The Greeks believed their gods lived in a big family on top of a mountain called Olympus. Most of the gods and goddesses looked like real people. Some were good and some bad. They loved to enjoy themselves. The chief god was called Zeus. This statue was discovered in the sea. Archaeologists think it may be a statue of Zeus.

The Greeks built temples for their gods to live in. This one was built for the goddess Athena of Athens.

This is how Athena was born. One day Zeus had a headache. To cure him another god hit him on the head with an axe! It was a strange thing to do. Then an even stranger thing happened. The goddess, Athena, was born out of a bump on Zeus' forehead. The Greeks made up many stories like this about their gods.

The Greeks tried to keep their gods happy and they took presents for the gods to the temple. This picture shows people making a **sacrifice** of an animal to the gods.

Heroes

▲ A vase showing Perseus attacking Medusa.

The Greeks also believed in people they called heroes. The heroes were not gods, they were humans who behaved and acted like gods. The heroes were brave and had exciting adventures.

The hero called Perseus killed a terrible monster. Her name was Medusa. If people looked at Medusa they were turned to stone.

The Underworld

The Greeks believed that dead people went to live in the **underworld.** The god, Hades, ruled in the underworld.

This picture shows Hades with Persephone. You can read their story on pages 20 and 21.

The body of a dead person was washed and perfumed. Then it was wrapped in material and flowers were put by the head. It was laid on a bed with its feet nearest the door because it was going on a journey.

A coin was placed under the dead person's tongue. It was meant for Charon, the ferryman, who took the dead across the River Styx to the Underworld.

◀ Charon and his ferry.

A Story from the Underworld

DEMETER was the goddess who looked after all the beautiful, growing things on earth. She had a lovely daughter called Kore.

Hades, the god of the underworld, saw Kore and thought how beautiful she was. He wanted her for his bride in the underworld. Hades decided to kidnap Kore and he took her across the River Styx to the underworld.

Demeter looked everywhere for Kore. She asked everyone if they had seen her daughter. She was miserable. Finally, she went to Helios, the Sun, and he told her that Hades had captured Kore and taken her to the underworld.

Demeter rushed to Zeus, the king of the gods, to ask him for help but he would not do anything. Demeter was so angry that she cursed the earth. Nothing would grow. There were no flowers, the trees died and there was nothing to eat. Zeus had to do something to help or the people on earth would all die.

In the underworld Hades was very kind to Kore. He tried to persuade her to eat something. This was because of a rule Zeus had made. If someone ate and drank anything in the underworld they were never allowed to leave. Hades offered Kore a fruit called a pomegranate and he tricked her into tasting a seed. Now she would have to stay with Hades in the underworld for ever.

Zeus decided to send a messenger to the underworld. This messenger flew as fast as he could with the wings on his boots. He was to tell Hades that he had to give up Kore. But he got there after Kore had tasted the pomegranate seed. He was too late.

The message came from the king of the gods and so Hades had to make an agreement with Zeus and Demeter. Kore had to spend three months of the year in the underworld as his queen and nine months of the year on earth with Demeter. When she was with Demeter she was called Kore and when she was in the underworld she was to be called Persephone.

When Persephone was in the underworld it was winter on earth. The skies were grey, the wind howled and the snow fell because Demeter was unhappy. But when she was with Demeter spring, summer and autumn came. Demeter was happy. Everything grew, the sun shone and the earth was beautiful once again.

Telling the Future

The Greeks believed that the gods sent messages to people about the future. The messages were called 'oracles'. Oracles were sent to priests and priestesses who then passed them on to ordinary people. People from all over Greece went to visit the famous priestesses at Delphi to find out about the future.

The priestess often answered questions with a puzzle. Once a king asked who would win a war. The priestess said war would make an empire fall. The king thought it meant he would beat his enemies. But in the war he was beaten and his empire fell.

▼ The ruins of the temple at Delphi.

▶ Someone asking the priestess a question.

ACTIVITIES

1 Look at the picture of the sacrifice on page 18. What do you think is happening to the animal? Can you describe the picture?

2 Why do you think the Greeks wanted to keep the gods happy?

3 Make up a play about Medusa. Some people could be turned to stone. How will Perseus kill Medusa?

4 The Greeks believed that the underworld was guarded by a fierce dog with seven heads called Cerberus. Sometimes bodies were buried with pieces of sweet honey cake in their hands. What do you think the cake was for?

5 Make a plasticine or clay model of Cerberus and Charon.

6 These Greek statues show Hades capturing Persephone.

Read the story of Hades and Persephone and draw pictures to tell the whole story. You can make it like a comic strip story.

7 Why do you think the priestess in Delphi answered questions with a riddle and did not tell people exactly what would happen? Where in a newspaper or magazine can you read about your future today? Do you believe people can tell the future?

The Wooden Horse

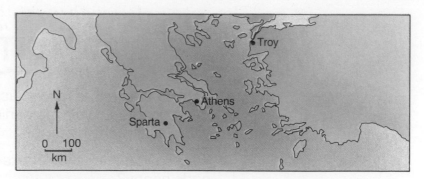

One of the most famous Greek stories is about the Wooden Horse. Queen Helen of Sparta ran away with Prince Paris to live in Troy. So a Greek army attacked Troy but its walls were so strong that they could not capture the city.

For ten years the Greeks camped outside the walls. Then they had the idea of building a wooden horse. Greek soldiers were hidden inside and the horse was left outside the city. The rest of the Greeks pretended to sail away.

This model shows what the wooden horse might have looked like.

The people of Troy thought the horse was a gift and pulled it into their city. They were really pleased with the horse. The Greek writer Euripides wrote hundreds of years later:

> The head was higher than the walls
> And O the size of the body!
> You couldn't move for people
> Cheering and singing and shouting . . .
> It was as big and black as a ship.

► The remains of the walls of Troy.

A young woman called Cassandra warned the people not to bring the horse in but they all ignored her. The Greeks climbed out of the horse at night and opened the city gates. The Greek army burst in, burned Troy and killed most of its people.

ACTIVITIES

1 Copy Euripides' poem and finish the story.

2 Archaeologists have found evidence that there was a war between Greece and Troy. But no-one is sure if the wooden horse was real, although it was a well-known Greek story. List the reasons you think it might be a legend. List the reasons you think it might be true.

3 Can you act out the story?

Sport, plays and music

Olympia

The Greeks loved sport. They thought their bodies should be fit and healthy.

Every four years games were held at Olympia. All the Greek cities came together to compete. The first games were held in 776 BC.

The games included running races, throwing the discus and javelin, wrestling, chariot racing, long jump and the pentathlon. Winners in the games were given a crown of laurel leaves. Women could not watch the men's games and they had their own festival where they ran running races.

▶ Statue of a discus thrower.

▼ The ruins of the racing track can still be seen at Olympia.

A temple for the god, Zeus, was built at Olympia. The sculptor, Pheidias, built a giant statue of Zeus for the temple. It was thirteen metres high. These ruins are all that are left of the temple.

This coin shows the statue.

This drawing shows what the archaeologists think the statue looked like when it was built.

A Greek writer described the temple and the statue. He wrote that the throne was decorated with gold, precious stones, ebony and ivory.

Near the temple archaeologists found bits of ivory and glass. They also found part of a pot mug with the words 'I belong to Pheidias' scratched onto it.

Theatre

Most Greek men loved to go to the theatre. The plays were part of a festival for the god of wine, Dionysos. To start with the plays were very short and there were just two actors. Longer plays were then written.

▲ These seats are in an open air theatre in Athens.

All Greek actors were men and they had to take the part of women. Some actors wore thick soles on their boots to make them bigger so that people could see them better. They wore brightly coloured clothes.

People went to the theatre for the whole day to see lots of plays. There was a competition to see which play was the best. One of the most clever writers was called Sophocles and his plays are still performed today.

Sophocles and other Greek writers wrote tragic plays. These plays were very exciting, often quite violent and always ended sadly. Some of the plays were about the gods and others were about the problems of rulers or of ordinary people.

There were also great comic writers, like Aristophanes, who wrote funny plays about the gods or about everyday life. One of the favourite characters was a naughty slave who was always getting into trouble.

Greek actors used masks to tell the audience if the character was old, young, ugly, beautiful, male or female.

▼ This actor is holding a mask.

▲ Actors used masks like these.

Music

There were many folk songs which the Greeks sang. There were songs to celebrate marriage, birth, the harvest, weaving, drinking and love. These were songs which everyone knew and enjoyed singing.

Some Greeks also played instruments. We do not know what the music sounded like because very little of it was written down. But we do know about the instruments from sculptures and vase paintings like this one.

ACTIVITIES

1 Look at the picture of the Olympic running track. What are the stone lines across the track for?

2 Whose mug was found near the ruins of the temple of Zeus?

3 How do we know what the temple and statue of Zeus looked like? What different kinds of evidence help us?

4 How are the modern day Olympic Games different? How are they the same?

5 Make your own masks showing different faces.

6 Look at the vase picture showing musical instruments. What kinds of instruments can you see?

Thinkers and inventors

The Greeks were always wondering about the things they saw around them. They were always asking questions and trying to find answers.

The men who looked for these answers were called **philosophers**. They studied history, mathematics, science and geography. They talked and wrote about politics and how people should live.

They drew maps and discovered that the world was round. Sometimes they were wrong. They thought that the sun, moon and planets all went round the earth.

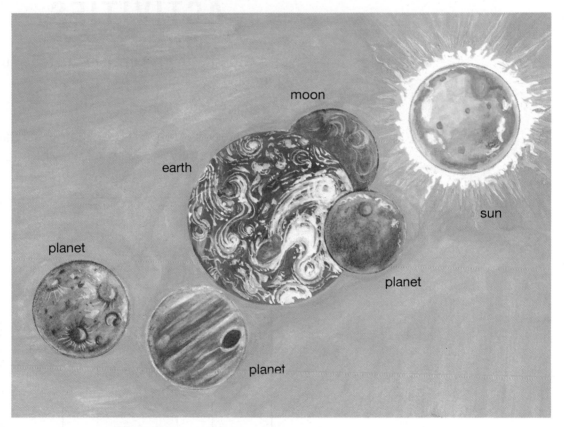

One Greek inventor was called Hero and he was the first person to discover the power of steam. It was many hundreds of years later that scientists found out again about steam.

One Greek philosopher, Diogenes, believed people should never enjoy themselves. So he lived in a barrel!

Archimedes was a clever thinker. One day he was sitting in his bath. He noticed that when he got into his bath the water spilled over the sides. He wondered why this happened and saw that it was because his body pushed it out. Different sizes of things pushed out different amounts of water.

He was so pleased that he had discovered this that he got out of his bath and ran down the road shouting 'Eureka! Eureka!' which means 'I've got it! I've got it!'

ACTIVITIES

1 What is wrong with the Greek idea of the sun, earth and planets?

2 Do you agree with Diogenes? Why?

3 Test Archimedes' idea. Fill a container to the top with water. Carefully put a small weight into the water. What happens?

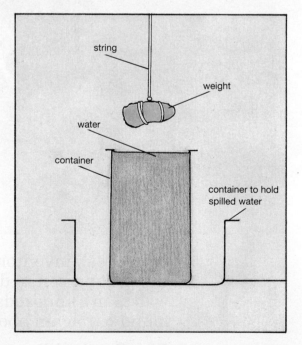

Try the experiment with different things. Each time measure the amount of water spilled.

Philip and Alexander

Do you remember that after the Greek war with Persia, Athens became very powerful? This made Sparta angry and there were many wars and quarrels between Athens and Sparta. There was one long war between 431 BC and 404 BC. At the end of the war no-one had really won but both cities were very weak after so much fighting. They could not fight any more.

It was soon after this that King Philip of Macedon decided to **invade** Greece. By 338 BC Philip and his son Alexander had **conquered** all of Greece. Philip was murdered but Alexander ruled Greece. Philip's grave was found by archaeologists. Scientists built up layers of clay on Philip's skull to show what he looked like when he was alive.

▶ Model of the face of Philip of Macedon.

Alexander was a great general and a brilliant fighter. He conquered a huge empire. In 333 BC he beat the King of Persia and went on to Egypt. Many stories were told about his bravery. Even his horse, Bucephalus, became famous. The horse was so wild that only Alexander could tame it. When the Greeks dared to rise against him they were defeated violently.

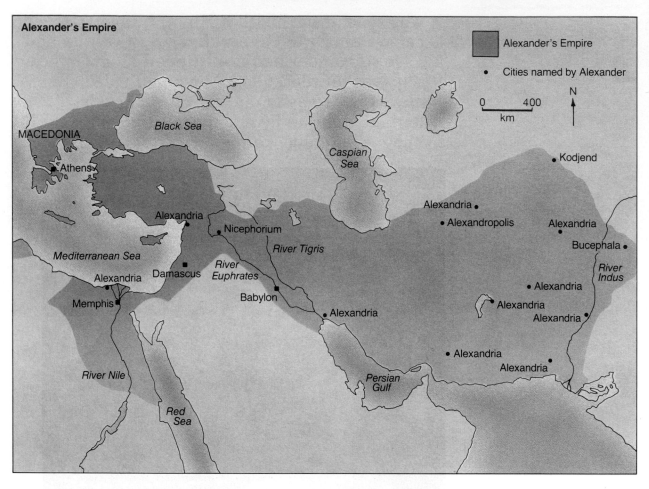

Alexander was also a very clever man. He was taught by a very famous Greek thinker called Aristotle. Greek ideas, Greek buildings and the Greek language spread into all the lands he conquered.

He became known as Alexander the Great and in Egypt he was called the son of Zeus. Alexander finally marched into India but he had to turn back. He died in 323 BC, still a young man.

This wall painting was found in an old Roman villa. It shows Alexander in battle with the Persian king. Alexander is on the left of the picture on horseback.

ACTIVITIES

1 Use your atlas and make a list of modern countries which would have been in Alexander's empire.

2 Why do you think Alexander beat the Greeks? Was there more than one reason?

3 Alexander was called 'The Great'. Do you think everyone thought he was 'great'? Who might disagree? Do you think he was a 'great' man?

4 How many towns were named after Alexander? Can you find out where they are? Where is the town named after his horse?

Romans and Greeks

After Alexander died his empire split up. Greece was ruled by the Macedonians. Once again the Greeks fought amongst themselves. At the same time the Romans were building up a new empire.

In 200 BC they began to show an interest in Greece. In 148 BC some Greek states joined together to fight the Romans but they were defeated. The rest of Greece was conquered in 146 BC. Greece was left to rule itself to start with but it became part of the Roman Empire.

► A Roman temple in France which was also part of the Roman Empire.

The Romans liked Greek buildings, temples and statues. They read the clever Greek writers and prayed to the Greek gods although they called them different names. They prayed to Zeus but called him Jupiter. All these ideas spread to other parts of the Roman empire.

At the same time many of the lands conquered by Alexander the Great kept their Greek ideas.

ACTIVITIES

1 Look at the picture of the Roman temple in France. Which building does it remind you of?

2 Can you find out which other countries became part of the Roman Empire? Do you think Greek ideas and buildings went to them as well?

The Greek Legacy

The Greeks left us The Olympic Games.

For many hundreds of years artists have learnt from Greek art. Many of them have copied Greek statues. This statue, David, is by a famous artist called Michaelangelo.
It was done in Italy in the sixteenth century.

They left behind many ideas about governments and about how we should live. Do you remember that Athens was a 'democracy' and many people voted?

IT'S **YOUR** VOTE

USE IT!

HOW TO VOTE

A lot of words we use today come from Greek words.

drama

theatre

music

comedy

tragedy

philosophy

politics

They also left us the idea of writing plays and going to the theatre. This scene shows some of London's theatres.

Builders have copied Greek ideas. One of the most famous examples of this is the British Museum in London.

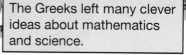

The Greeks left many clever ideas about mathematics and science.

ACTIVITIES

1 Think about the different things the Greeks have left us. Which is most important? Put them in order and give reasons. Do you all agree?

2 The Greeks lived thousands of years ago. How do we know about them? Write down all the different kinds of evidence you found in this book.

Glossary

ancient	Something very old, from a very long time ago.
archaeologist	Someone who studies the past, usually by digging things up.
B.C.	Before Christ.
chitons	Greeks' tunics.
city states	The area around a city ruled by one government.
colonies	New lands where the people from Greece settled.
conquer	To defeat and take control.
democracy	Government by the people, or by people elected to rule.
empire	A group of countries ruled by one person or one government.
evidence	Something left from the past – includes writing, buildings, art. If we look at them carefully they can give us proof about the past.
government	System by which the people are ruled.
himation	Greek cloak.
invade	To enter with an army.
legacy	Something left behind – what the Greeks handed down.
philosophers	People who think and write about ideas, beliefs and science.
sacrifice	Killing an animal to please the gods.
slaves	People owned by others. They have to work for their masters and are not free to do what they want.
trade	Buying and selling goods, exchanging one thing for another.
underworld	The place where the Greeks believed the dead went to live.

Index

Acknowledgements

Ancient Art and Architecture Collection p4 (bottom left), p5 (bottom left), p8, p10 (inset), p12, p13 (all three), p15 (bottom right), p19 (bottom left), p26 (bottom), p29 (both). Architectural Association p36 (Caroline Hambury), p38 (bottom left) (G. Philip Bell). Barnaby's Picture Library p37 (bottom), British Museum p2 (both), p14 (top & bottom left), p15 (top left), p18 (bottom), p30. Claus & Liselotte Hansmann p22 (inset), p23. Michael Holford p7, p14 (bottom right), p15 (top right), p19 (top). Olly Hatch p38 (top). Manchester Museum/John Prag p33. Mansell Collection p15 (bottom left). SCALA p17 (both), p18 (top), p26 (top), p27 (top left), p28, p35. Sonia Halliday Photographs p5 (top), p10, p22, p24 (both). Telegraph Colour Library p3, p27 (top right), p37 (top).